# THE APPLICATION

### A Couples Guide and Workbook

*To a Healthy, Happy, Successful Relationship & Marriage*

## Dr. Toni Sims Muhammad

All rights reserved. No part of this publication may be used or reproduced in any manner whatsoever without the written permission of the Publisher. Printed in the United States of America. For information email us at: Vanguard Educational Services Academic Press, vangaurdedsrv@gmail.com.

## A NOTE TO READERS

This publication is sold with the understanding that it is not meant to offer or replace medical or psychological advice. Moreover, the general situations described in this book may not apply to your particular circumstances. Therefore, no medical or mental health action in this book should be taken without seeking the advice or counsel of trained medical or mental health professionals. This book is not intended to diagnose, prescribe or be a substitute for physician advice or otherwise.

Copyright © 2012, 2013 Toni Sims Muhammad

All rights reserved.

ISBN-10: 0615631606
ISBN-13: 978-0615631608

# *Foreword*

Years ago, when I was in college, I overheard this young lady telling a guy real loudly, I'm not taking applications but I'll campaign for you." I remember thinking wow, what an awesome concept that instead of just meeting someone and "hooking up" what if you could have them to just submit a "dating" application. To some people this may seem absurd, but to me it made perfect sense. Of course, I did nothing with the thought except to remember it when someone uninteresting attempted to flirt with me. It worked too!

Fast forward years later and it became obvious to me that an application is exactly what people needed. One day, I was playing around and actually came up with the first questions for a dating/courtship application. The next day, I went to one of my Marriage and Family classes and made a grand announcement, "I did it!" The students were excited and wanted a copy of the application immediately. I began to share bits and pieces in my lectures. Years later, students approached me and said, "hey can I get a copy of that courtship application," or "that application was helpful," or better still, "I wish I had listened to you and tried that application." Many of them realized that dating, courtship and finding the right mate is very hard. And no one was offering them a more personalized and intimate way to navigate the process so that they would not waste their time.

Thus, if you are looking for a mate, a helpmeet, and someone special to spend the rest of your life with, *The Application* is for you!

All of the questions, originated from my educational background and experiences, things I wanted to know, things I wished I had asked before I married the first time. The questions are truly my own. Therefore, I hope this helpful little application will guide you through a constructive and successful process of discovery to find out what you really need to know about yourself and someone you are considering for a mate.

## CONTENTS

Foreword

Acknowledgments

| | |
|---|---:|
| **Part ONE – Five Important Perspectives** | 1 |
| **ONE: Courtship Versus Dating** | 3 |
| **TWO: Being Equally Yoked!!!** | 4 |
| **THREE: Time Together or Apart?** | 7 |
| **FOUR: Patience & Your True Mate** | 8 |
| **FIVE: Self-Esteem, Self Love & the Other!** | 10 |
| **Research** | 14 |
| **Part FOUR - The Courtship Application** | 39 |
| **The Application Instructions** | 40 |
| **The Application** | 45 |
| **Epilogue** | 95 |
| **Definition of Terms** | 97 |
| **Suggested Book Readings** | 100 |
| **Notes** | 101 |

# ACKNOWLEDGMENTS

I must thank all of my students. I dare not attempt to name you all because I do not want to leave any of you out. Thank you for allowing me the opportunity to teach marriage and the family for over 20 years. You all have taught me so much and I am forever indebted to you.

I also want to thank all of the couples who have been direct and indirect inspirations for this book. Dexter & Dr. Danita, Benny & Angela Faye, Reverend John & Tatiana, Dr. Charles & Rita, Dr. Umar & Yvonne, Joe & Dr. Rhonda, Lee & Gertrude, Lorenzo & Matilda, Sylvester & Sandra, Lee & Lolita, Bun & Sonia, Darryl & LaShonda, Robert & Andrea, Savon & Dr. Jacqueline, Harith & Josie, Shahid & Khadijah, Darryl & Deborah, Dan & Portia, Clarence & Melinda, Stephanie & Louis, Willie & Michelle, Walter & Phyllis, Troy & Deborah, Darryl & Kim, Sidney & Estefania, Ghani & DeeAngela, and Kareem & Betty.

I must also acknowledge Marva, Tara, Bridgett, Melanie, Celesia and countless other sisters for "putting up with me" over the years and for their feedback and assistance with this work.

I extend a special thank you to my Minister and his beautiful Wife and Companion Mother Khadijah -- your example has guided me throughout my stages of growth and development.

To Tynetta, Ava, Amir and Kaeed, you have contributed to this work in ways that you have yet to understand. Your inspiration is truly the gift that keeps on giving.

Finally, I must give special acknowledgment to my husband, Tarik, my first and hopefully last applicant. Thank you for always giving so much of yourself to us and our children.

# Part ONE – Five Important Perspectives

TONI SIMS MUHAMMAD

## ONE: Courtship Versus Dating

Courtship (the deliberative process and act of seeking evidence, proof and information that proves or disproves one's motive, intention and purpose) is what is missing for many couples looking for a mate. Many have been convinced by conventional social norms that dating is the way...the best way to find a mate. Well, here are some myths about dating:

- Dating will lead to marriage.
- The longer you Date the better your chances for marriage.
- Dating Couples have better marriages that last longer.
- Dating Couples better understand their mate's sexual desires.
- Dating Couples have more fun.
- Dating Couples have fewer expenses.
- Dating Couples are mutually exclusive.
- Dating Couples get to know each other very well and therefore argue less.

*Share your thoughts, experiences...*

_____

_____

_____

_____

## TWO: Being Equally Yoked

Today, we take this important spiritual concept far too lightly.

Granted, there are times when we are in such a hurry to have someone in our life that we rush to make decisions and choices about people who may not be the person that God intends for us.

There was a time when I thought, that if someone had money, a car, a nice body, nice clothes and shoes, a high status career, and even a college degree, that these things would be what I needed and enough.

A great thing happened on the way to my life purpose; I found that any old person would not do. Not that God makes junk. However, that God had already chosen a divine, appointed and anointed person for me. And until that person was made manifest, God, in all wisdom had already bestowed upon me all the love I needed at that stage of my development. I began to realize and to know that as long as I was willing to be found working that purpose and plan for my life, that God could and would bring my divine mate forward.

## THE APPLICATION

So what is being equally yoked? Moreover, what does yoke have to do with it? Being equally yoked is when you hurt; your mate hurts not out of sympathy (to feel sorry for) but out of empathy (to truly understand).

Being equally yoked is when you can truly share the same ideas and beliefs and you do not have to take time to explain the basics about your spiritual ideas and values. Being equally yoked is striving for your purpose and your mate does not demand that they be a part of what you are doing...because they are working out God's plan for them.

When two people come together, it should ultimately be to assist and serve one another towards God's plan and purpose for their lives as individuals and together. And, being equally yoked has everything to do with it.

See I know me. And you had better know you. Because, if you are a "deep" person, than you need and deserve to be married to a deep person. Especially for women, this is so important. Because if you expect a man to serve as head of the household, he has to be wise and he has to know how to pierce your soul. That will require great knowledge of God's word, himself, the nature of God's woman, the times we live in and the proper handling of people.

The woman of God has to have the man of God and nothing less. The man of God possesses spiritual traits and characteristics that lead to social, cultural, and economic success. Spiritually, he acts in accordance with what he believes and what he knows to be the truth of God's way and word. Socially, he strives for refinement, culture and civilization when interacting with his fellow human beings. Economically, he understands the dynamics and principles of supply and demand as well as the people activity necessary to produce lucrative and responsible exchanges.

Therefore, you must not marry or be with someone, for the 'wrong' reasons. And if you do, you will deal with the consequences. Again, do not marry for sex, for money, for degrees, to impress friends, to show off, for looks, just to say, "I have somebody, now what!" Marry because you are equally yoked.

To save the family, we can no longer just get together and marry for the wrong reasons, out of season, and with no purpose.

*Share your thoughts, experiences...*

_____

_____

_____

## THREE: Time Together or Apart

That's right...absence *does* make the heart grow fonder. If it were up to me, which it is, I would advise all couples to "get away" whether in the bedroom, the house, take a day vacation, and visit friends out of state...live life to the fullest. You are not joined at the hip...where you should be joined is in spirit.

Often times, couples mistake physical intimacy for genuine love and happiness. However, it is when we are away from each other that we can truly appreciate who we are, what we bring to a relationship, who the other person is, and what they bring to the relationship.

*Share your thoughts, experiences...*

_____

_____

_____

## FOUR: Patience & Your True Mate

Life is full of many awesome adventures, but I must say that the biggest adventure for many people is meeting their true mate. Sometimes we look so hard for something and it is right in front of our faces. Other times, we are just in all the wrong places.

Yet what is most compelling in our quest to have our true mate is the fact that we may not be fulfilling our purpose in life. When we live to fulfill our purpose in life...our mission that is connected to the higher self and the God in us, we meet our divine mate.

So often, we think it is the other way around and that is not it at all. It is finding out why God put us on this earth, striving to be in accord with that purpose and mission, and working to fulfill that purpose and mission that aligns us with God's desire for us to do his will...not alone, but with our true mate!

*So ask yourself this...* What is God's purpose for my life?

Am I living my purpose and mission in accord with God's divine plan? (His divine plan for humanity is peace...freedom, justice and equality). Will my potential mate support, add to or help me through this journey called life towards God's divine plan?

## THE APPLICATION

If your answer is not clear and rooted in positive conscious thought then continue to strive towards finding God's purpose for your life -- not a mate!

Be patient and before you know it... You will meet your mate!

*Share your thoughts, experiences...*

_____

_____

_____

## FIVE: Self-Esteem, Self Love & the Other

Self-esteem is hard to come by, especially when we constantly seek others to give us what we want and need, but already should have. No one can or will give you everything you want and need but you!

The key to any healthy relationship is the ability to have and maintain the correct self-outlook and self-reflection. We must constantly look in the mirrors of our mind, and soul, to find what makes us who we are, and why we make the choices, we make.

Unfortunately, we come to relationships expecting. We expect to be made whole, happy, peaceful, fulfilled and ultimately accepted and loved. We expect the person to be there for life through our pitfalls and downfalls. However, what we must bring to the relationship is the ability to accept. We must be able to accept the truth about ourselves and the other person and allow that person and ourselves to change and grow.

If change and growth means they act up, act out and leave then so be it. Our job is to recognize that true self-esteem, self-love comes from within, and until we actually learn to

THE APPLICATION

workout our self-love and self-esteem muscles, we will always find ourselves dependent on the other!

*What are your thoughts, experiences...*

_____

_____

**TONI SIMS MUHAMMAD**

# PART TWO - COUPLE WORK

*Research*

## Find popular articles about:

- "Roles" of Woman and Man in a Marriage/Family
- Fighting Fair/Domestic Abuse/Emotional Abuse/Verbal Abuse
- Sexuality/Sexual Fulfillment
- Rearing Children
- Money & Finances (Family Sustainability)

These hot button topics/issues always seem to come up in a relationship/marriage. This exercise is intended to orientate you to "what's going on" in the world of popular research and give you refreshing perspectives about couples today. If you find more than one article that you like, then share it with your potential mate as well.

**Alternative watch sitcoms or movies instead. {HINT: make it fun, have dinner and a movie night, invite other couples}**

Some of my favorites include:

- My Wife and Kids
- Everybody Loves Raymond
- Everybody Hates Chris
- George Lopez Show
- Cheaper by the Dozen
- Tyler Perry's Why Did I Get Married

A Couples Guide and Workbook

## Assignment 1

## Article that explores the Roles of Woman and Man in a Marriage/Family

1. Title of the Article: _____

2. Date of the Article: _____

3. How would you rate the article?

_____Excellent   _____Good   _____Okay   _____ Bad   _____Terrible

4. Identify a few important points, aspects of the article.

_____   _____

_____   _____

*5. Share the Article with your potential mate.*

6. How did your potential mate rate the article?

_____Excellent   _____Good   _____Okay   _____ Bad   _____Terrible

The Application

7. Compare and contrast the important points, aspects of the article you identified with your mates response(s).

8. Were your responses similar _____ different_____ (or) both _____?
   - Identify what accounts for your perspectives (whether similar, different or both).
   _____

   _____

   _____

9. If your responses were different, can they be reconciled?

   ____ Yes  ____ No  ____ Maybe

If yes, how can they be reconciled?
_____

_____

If no, how can there be understanding and acceptance of the difference(s)?
_____

A Couples Guide and Workbook

_____

Did you and your potential mate reach a FINAL Agreement and/or Understanding about this article? _____Yes _____No

*If yes, proceed to the next article assignment.*

*If no, return immediately to the beginning of the process and START OVER. DO NOT proceed to the next article assignment.*

Are you and your potential mate prepared to move on to the next article? _____Yes _____No

*If yes, proceed to the next article assignment.*

*If no, return immediately to the beginning of the process and START OVER. DO NOT proceed to the next article assignment.*

-----------------------------------------

**Assignment 2**

**Article that explores Fighting Fair/Domestic Violence/Emotional Abuse/Verbal Abuse**

1. Title of the Article: _____

2. Date of the Article: _____

The Application

3. How would you rate the article?

\_\_\_\_\_Excellent      \_\_\_\_\_Good      \_\_\_\_\_Okay      \_\_\_\_\_ Bad      \_\_\_\_\_Terrible

4. Identify a few important points, aspects of the article.

_____      _____

_____      _____

*5. Share the Article with your potential mate.*

6. How did your potential mate rate the article?

\_\_\_\_\_Excellent      \_\_\_\_\_Good      \_\_\_\_\_Okay      \_\_\_\_\_ Bad      \_\_\_\_\_Terrible

7. Compare and contrast the important points, aspects of the article you identified with your mates response(s).

8. Were your responses similar \_\_\_\_\_ different_____ (or) both _____?

- Identify what accounts for your perspectives (whether similar, different or both).

_____

_____

_____

9. If your responses were different, can they be reconciled?

____ Yes  ____ No  ____ Maybe

If yes, how can they be reconciled?
_____

_____

If no, how can there be understanding and acceptance of the difference(s)?
_____

_____

Did you and your potential mate reach a FINAL Agreement and/or Understanding about this article? ____Yes ____No

*If yes, proceed to the next article assignment.*

*If no, return immediately to the beginning of the process and START OVER. DO NOT proceed to the next article assignment.*

Are you and your potential mate prepared to move on to the next article? ____Yes ____No

The Application

*If yes, proceed to the next article assignment.*

*If no, return immediately to the beginning of the process and START OVER. DO NOT proceed to the next article assignment.*

-------------------------------------

**Assignment 3**

**Article that explores Sexuality and Sexual Fulfillment**

1. Title of the Article: _____

2. Date of the Article: _____

3. How would you rate the article?

_____Excellent   _____Good   _____Okay   _____ Bad   _____Terrible

4. Identify a few important points, aspects of the article.

_____   _____

_____   _____

*5. Share the Article with your potential mate.*

6. How did your potential mate rate the article?

_____Excellent   _____Good   _____Okay   _____Bad   _____Terrible

7. Compare and contrast the important points, aspects of the article you identified with your mates response(s).

8. Were your responses similar _____ different_____ (or) both _____?

- Identify what accounts for your perspectives (whether similar, different or both).

_____

_____

_____

9. If your responses were different, can they be reconciled?

____ Yes   ____ No   ____ Maybe

If yes, how can they be reconciled?

_____

The Application

_____

If no, how can there be understanding and acceptance of the difference(s)?
_____

_____

Did you and your potential mate reach a FINAL Agreement and/or Understanding about this article? ____Yes _____No

*If yes, proceed to the next article assignment.*

*If no, return immediately to the beginning of the process and START OVER. DO NOT proceed to the next article assignment.*

Are you and your potential mate prepared to move on to the next article? ____Yes _____No

*If yes, proceed to the next article assignment.*

*If no, return immediately to the beginning of the process and START OVER. DO NOT proceed to the next article assignment.*

A Couples Guide and Workbook

---

## Assignment 4

## Article that explores Rearing Children

1. Title of the Article: _____

2. Date of the Article: _____

3. How would you rate the article?

_____Excellent  _____Good  _____Okay  _____ Bad  _____Terrible

4. Identify a few important points, aspects of the article.

_____   _____

_____   _____

*5. Share the Article with your potential mate.*

6. How did your potential mate rate the article?

The Application

_____Excellent     _____Good     _____Okay     _____Bad     _____Terrible

7. Compare and contrast the important points, aspects of the article you identified with your mates response(s).



8. Were your responses similar _____ different _____ (or) both _____ ?

- Identify what accounts for your perspectives (whether similar, different or both).
_____


_____


_____


9. If your responses were different, can they be reconciled?

____ Yes ____ No ____ Maybe


If yes, how can they be reconciled?
_____


_____

If no, how can there be understanding and acceptance of the difference(s)?
_____

_____

Did you and your potential mate reach a FINAL Agreement and/or Understanding about this article? _____Yes _____No

*If yes, proceed to the next article assignment.*

*If no, return immediately to the beginning of the process and START OVER. DO NOT proceed to the next article assignment.*

Are you and your potential mate prepared to move on to the next article? _____Yes _____No

*If yes, proceed to the next article assignment.*

*If no, return immediately to the beginning of the process and START OVER. DO NOT proceed to the next article assignment.*

-----------------------------------------

**Assignment 5**

**Article that explores Money & Finances (Family Sustainability)**

1. Title of the Article: _____

2. Date of the Article: _____

The Application

3. How would you rate the article?

_____Excellent     _____Good     _____Okay     _____ Bad     _____Terrible

4. Identify a few important points, aspects of the article.

_____      _____

_____      _____

*5. Share the Article with your potential mate.*

6. How did your potential mate rate the article?

_____Excellent     _____Good     _____Okay     _____ Bad     _____Terrible

7. Compare and contrast the important points, aspects of the article you identified with your mates response(s).

8. Were your responses similar _____ different_____ (or) both _____?
- Identify what accounts for your perspectives (whether similar, different or both).

_____

_____

A Couples Guide and Workbook

_____

9. If your responses were different, can they be reconciled?

____ Yes ____ No ____ Maybe

If yes, how can they be reconciled?
_____

_____

If no, how can there be understanding and acceptance of the difference(s)?
_____

_____

Did you and your potential mate reach a FINAL Agreement and/or Understanding about this article? ____Yes _____No

If yes, proceed to the **Final Interview Process**.

If no, find another article and review. If you are unable to reach consensus, go to **Part III – The Decision**. Determine if you are willing to proceed or terminate the process until you reach consensus or you can agree to disagree respectfully.

# The Application

# THE FINAL INTERVIEW

## Couple Immersion

Identify at least **5** couples that you know are willing to host you and your soon to be spouse for casual informal get together.  *(At least two of the couples should be family related.)*

_____     _____

_____     _____

_____     _____

_____     _____

_____     _____

**Journal:** Write down notes about Family/Friends/Associates responses and reactions to your potential mate (For example, what characteristics about the person did you observe about their interactions - were they cordial, friendly, too friendly, easy to talk too, withdrawn, engaging, entertaining, interesting, warm, kind, harsh, standoffish, flirtatious, helpful, talkative, shy).

The Application

*These surveys can assist you with the final interview and determination process.*

| (Family & Friends) Character Assessment | | | | | | | | |
|---|---|---|---|---|---|---|---|---|
| **Traits** | Family | | | | Friends/Associates | | | |
| **Honesty** | Yes | Unsure | Some What | No | Yes | Unsure | Some What | No |
| **Fairness** | Yes | Unsure | Some What | No | Yes | Unsure | Some What | No |
| **Integrity** | Yes | Unsure | Some What | No | Yes | Unsure | Some What | No |
| **Attention to Details** | Yes | Unsure | Some What | No | Yes | Unsure | Some What | No |
| **Flexibility** | Yes | Unsure | Some What | No | Yes | Unsure | Some What | No |
| **Willingness to Reciprocate** | Yes | Unsure | Some What | No | Yes | Unsure | Some What | No |
| **Generosity** | Yes | Unsure | Some What | No | Yes | Unsure | Some What | No |
| **Ability to Listen** | Yes | Unsure | Some What | No | Yes | Unsure | Some What | No |
| **Calm under pressure** | Yes | Unsure | Some What | No | Yes | Unsure | Some What | No |
| **Helpfulness** | Yes | Unsure | Some What | No | Yes | Unsure | Some What | No |
| **Respectful** | Yes | Unsure | Some What | No | Yes | Unsure | Some What | No |
| **Sense of Humor** | Yes | Unsure | Some What | No | Yes | Unsure | Some What | No |
| **Punctual** | Yes | Unsure | Some What | No | Yes | Unsure | Some What | No |
| **Emotional Stability** | Yes | Unsure | Some What | No | Yes | Unsure | Some What | No |
| **Grooming/Hygiene** | Yes | Unsure | Some What | No | Yes | Unsure | Some What | No |
| **Affectionate/Compassionate** | Yes | Unsure | Some What | No | Yes | Unsure | Some What | No |
| **Intelligence** | Yes | Unsure | Some What | No | Yes | Unsure | Some What | No |
| **Introspection** | Yes | Unsure | Some What | No | Yes | Unsure | Some What | No |
| **Communication** | Yes | Unsure | Some What | No | Yes | Unsure | Some What | No |
| **Commitment (Loyalty)** | Yes | Unsure | Some What | No | Yes | Unsure | Some What | No |

*Observe and assess how your potential mate acts, reacts, interacts to family and friends.*

# The Application

*How to Score:  Yes (3 points); Unsure (2); Somewhat (1); No (0)*

*Total Points =* _____

___

60 – 54 points = 100% - 90% rating (Excellent Highest Expectation):  Demonstrates all or most endearing and enduring traits considered vital and essential for positive relationship dynamics.

53 – 48 points = 89 - 80% rating (Above Expectation Average):  Demonstrates many endearing and enduring traits considered vital and essential for positive relationship dynamics. Supplemental knowledge necessary to increase improvement in areas.

47 – 42 points = 79 - 70% rating (Average Expectation):  Demonstrates some endearing traits considered vital and essential for positive relationship dynamics but needs more traits that are enduring rooted in knowledge, maturity and/or experiences that reinforce and maintain positive relationship dynamics.

41 – Below points = 69% - lower ratings (Below Expectation):  Demonstrates a few and insufficient endearing and enduring traits considered vital and essential for positive relationship dynamics. Possible reasons might include lacks knowledge, maturity and/or experiences that create, build and foster these characteristics.

Discuss the assessment and score with your potential mate.

| (YOUR) Final Interview Character Assessment |||||||||
|---|---|---|---|---|---|---|---|---|
| **Traits** | **Public** |||| **Private** ||||
| **Honesty** | Yes | Unsure | Some What | No | Yes | Unsure | Some What | No |
| **Fairness** | Yes | Unsure | Some What | No | Yes | Unsure | Some What | No |
| **Integrity** | Yes | Unsure | Some What | No | Yes | Unsure | Some What | No |
| **Attention to Details** | Yes | Unsure | Some What | No | Yes | Unsure | Some What | No |
| **Flexibility** | Yes | Unsure | Some What | No | Yes | Unsure | Some What | No |
| **Willingness to Reciprocate** | Yes | Unsure | Some What | No | Yes | Unsure | Some What | No |
| **Generosity** | Yes | Unsure | Some What | No | Yes | Unsure | Some What | No |
| **Ability to Listen** | Yes | Unsure | Some What | No | Yes | Unsure | Some What | No |
| **Calm under pressure** | Yes | Unsure | Some What | No | Yes | Unsure | Some What | No |
| **Helpfulness** | Yes | Unsure | Some What | No | Yes | Unsure | Some What | No |
| **Respectful** | Yes | Unsure | Some What | No | Yes | Unsure | Some What | No |
| **Sense of Humor** | Yes | Unsure | Some What | No | Yes | Unsure | Some What | No |
| **Punctual** | Yes | Unsure | Some What | No | Yes | Unsure | Some What | No |
| **Emotional Stability** | Yes | Unsure | Some What | No | Yes | Unsure | Some What | No |
| **Grooming/Hygiene** | Yes | Unsure | Some What | No | Yes | Unsure | Some What | No |
| **Affectionate/Compassionate** | Yes | Unsure | Some What | No | Yes | Unsure | Some What | No |
| **Intelligence** | Yes | Unsure | Some What | No | Yes | Unsure | Some What | No |
| **Introspection** | Yes | Unsure | Some What | No | Yes | Unsure | Some What | No |
| **Communication** | Yes | Unsure | Some What | No | Yes | Unsure | Some What | No |
| **Commitment (Loyalty)** | Yes | Unsure | Some What | No | Yes | Unsure | Some What | No |

*Assess how your potential mate acts, reacts, and interacts to YOU in private and public settings.*

# The Application

*How to Score: Yes (3 points); Unsure (2); Somewhat (1); No (0)*

*Total Points =* _____

---

60 – 54 points = 100% - 90% rating (Excellent Highest Expectation): Demonstrates all or most endearing and enduring traits considered vital and essential for positive relationship dynamics.

53 – 48 points = 89 - 80% rating (Above Expectation Average): Demonstrates many endearing and enduring traits considered vital and essential for positive relationship dynamics. Supplemental knowledge necessary to increase improvement in areas.

47 – 42 points = 79 - 70% rating (Average Expectation): Demonstrates some endearing traits considered vital and essential for positive relationship dynamics but needs more traits that are enduring rooted in knowledge, maturity and/or experiences that reinforce and maintain positive relationship dynamics.

41 – Below points = 69% - lower ratings (Below Expectation): Demonstrates a few and insufficient endearing and enduring traits considered vital and essential for positive relationship dynamics. Possible reasons might include lacks knowledge, maturity and/or experiences that create, build and foster these characteristics.

Discuss the assessment and score with your potential mate.

# PART THREE – THE DECISION

# The Application

**THE DECISION**

When you are ready, contact your potential mate and inform them of your intention to terminate the courtship or to move forward in the courtship toward engagement.

**REASONS FOR TERMINATION**

During this process, as well as after completing the application, these may be reasons to consider terminating a courtship:

- You do not like (find agreement with) the responses provided by the potential mate (more than 20% of the application).
- You are uncomfortable with the response provided by the potential mate.
- You find that the potential mate's responses lack sufficient explanation and details (more than 20% of the application).
- You find that the potential mate responses dramatically differ from yours. This is also, what I refer to as the push/pull dynamic or *the ability to expand and contract* in a relationship -- very essential to longevity (more than 20% of the application).

Regardless if the courtship termination decision is mutual or one-sided, it may be best and even safer to severe the courtship over the phone.  You may feel bold and perhaps have some things you want to express to the individual; however, attempting to "get it off your chest" in person may not be wise.

In recent years, I have known of several unfortunate 'breakups" that have led to violence, the threat of violence and even death.  So why risk it.  Just be safe because you do not need to experiment with your life to make a point.

Moreover, meeting with a person, face to face to "break-up" can create awkward and difficult challenges for sharing your thoughts, ideas, and concerns to terminate the courtship. Each person should enter and leave this process knowing that neither of you owe the other person *nothing.*  You came to the process of "free will" and you should be allowed to leave on the same basis.

**TOWARD ENGAGEMENT**

If you have made it through the *Important Perspectives* discussion, the *Couple Work*, the *Final Interviews,* and respond with a resounding certainty to the following, this may mean that you are:

## The Application

- Clear about who this person is (at this stage),
- Clear about who this person may potentially become,
- Able to accept the person for the good,
- Able to accept the person for the bad,
- Able to accept the whole person for the beautiful and the ugly,
- Willing to make a lifelong commitment to this person,
- Willing to make a lifelong commitment to this person's family (in laws, siblings),
- Willing to make a lifelong commitment to this person's children (under 16).

***CONGRATULATIONS!***

***You have completed a major phase and process toward TRUE COMMITMENT.***

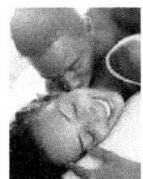

*Now The APPLICATION!*

# Part FOUR - The Courtship Application

## The Application Instructions

**Instructions:** This application for courtship is invasive. It contains over 200 items, though it is not exhaustive. It requires introspection and honesty if you are seriously ready to "go to court" and possibly marry. If you are not seriously ready to marry *(i.e., be introspective and honest with someone you desire to marry)* then **DO NOT** begin this application and immediately withdraw from any courtship unless and until you are ready to do so.

***FIRST***

Please give your potential mate at least <u>two weeks</u> to adequately respond to every question, gather information and complete the writing portion of this application. You may give additional time as necessary.

## SECOND

Once you and your potential mate complete the application, you should arrange a series of face to face meeting to:

- *1st,* discuss your reaction to completing the application. (Nervousness, Excitement, Unsure)
- *2nd*, share your responses to **EACH** question in an informal interview. This stage can take as long as you and your potential mate desire. **CAUTION:** *This is an interview, not an interrogation.* If you feel uncomfortable during any stage of the interview, then immediately **STOP** until you can maintain composure and control.
    - If you still are uncomfortable discussing your potential mate's background and responses on the Application then you are not ready for ***everything*** this person may bring to a relationship.
- *3rd,* provide your partner with a copy of your completed application for their independent review.

## THIRD

Meet with your potential mate again and reconcile any concerns about the application and interview. It may take weeks or even months to go through the entire application process. That is fine. Take your time. You may be about to make a life altering and life long decision.

The Application

**FOURTH**

Once you have completed the process, spend some time in silence and meditate (reflect) on what you are learning about yourself and your courtship partner. You may pray, read scripture or other positive and helpful books during this time. You may also seek counsel from a trusted, non-judgmental confident, a pastor or certified counselor. *Be careful. Do not share "the details" with family and friends who may intentionally or unintentionally use that information and interject themselves into the process.* **After serious deliberation of all the information available to you, process what you have learned about yourself and your courtship partner and make a decision to engage or terminate.**

## Illustration 1. Application Process

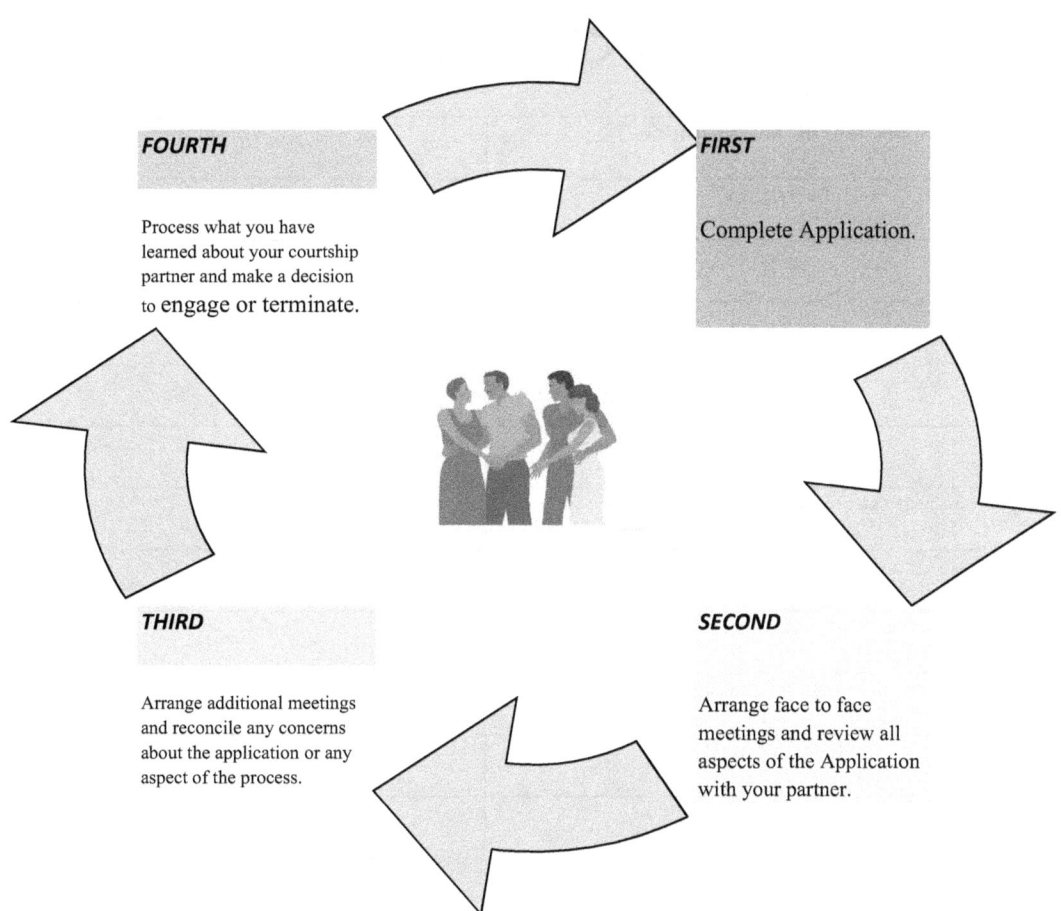

**FIRST**
Complete Application.

**SECOND**
Arrange face to face meetings and review all aspects of the Application with your partner.

**THIRD**
Arrange additional meetings and reconcile any concerns about the application or any aspect of the process.

**FOURTH**
Process what you have learned about your courtship partner and make a decision to engage or terminate.

# A Checklist

| Sections of the Application | Completed |
|:---:|:---:|
| Background | |
| Leisure | |
| Financial | |
| Education | |
| Family | |
| Marital/Childrearing Perspectives | |
| Spirituality/Beliefs | |
| Criminal Record | |
| Emotional Stability | |
| Health/Sexuality | |
| Writing Activity | |

# The Application

The Application

A Couples Guide and Workbook

**APPLICANT BACKGROUND**

1. First Name_____

2. Middle _____

3. Last Name _____

4. Address _____

5. City_____ State _____ Zip _____

6. Phone # _____

a. Email #1 _____  b. Email #2 _____

7. Ethnicity_____  8. Date of Birth _____

9. City/State you were born in_____

The Application

10. Occupation(s)_____

_____

*(Be prepared to provide a detailed work history for at least the past 3 years.)*


11. Do you live alone?   _____Yes   _____No


a. If no, who do you live with?  ___ roommate  ___parent  ___sibling  ___other _____


12. Do you travel?  _____Yes  _____No   a. How often? _____


13. Name some places you have visited:

_____     _____

_____     _____


14. Where would you consider or like to live or move?

_____     _____

_____    _____


15. Are there any circumstances or reasons you would consider relocating?

_____


**ASK Your Own Question(s)**


1._____


2._____

-----------------------------------

# Leisure

1. What is your favorite color? _____

2. Do you like to watch sports on television? ____Yes  ____ Sometimes ____No

3. Favorite Sport Event(s)

_____   _____


_____   _____


4. What are some of your favorite foods? *(if you are a vegetarian please check here_____)*


_____   _____


_____   _____


_____   _____

5. Do you like to eat out (at restaurants)? _____Yes  _____ Sometimes ____No

a. If no, why not? _____

6. If yes, name some restaurants you like to eat at:

_____        _____

_____        _____

_____        _____

7. Do you like to go to the movies? _____Yes  _____ Sometimes _____No

8. Name recent movies you have seen:

_____        _____

_____        _____

_____        _____

The Application

9. Do you like having "get together" with family or friends?

___Yes  ____ Sometimes ____No

a. If no, why not? _____

10. Can you dance? _____Yes  _____ Sometimes _____No

11. Can you sing? _____Yes  _____ Sometimes _____No

a. What kind of music do you like?

_____   _____

_____   _____

12. Can you draw? _____Yes  _____ Sometimes _____No

13. Please indicate any other hobbies that you have:

_____   _____

_____   _____

14. Do you schedule time for yourself? _____Yes _____ Sometimes _____No

a. What do you do? _____
_____

b. Describe an evening alone with you:
_____
_____

15. Do you like nature (out doors)? _____Yes _____ Sometimes _____No

16. Can you swim? _____Yes _____No   a. If no, do you want to learn? _____Yes _____No

**ASK Your Own Question(s)**

1._____

2._____

# The Application

## Financial

1. Do you work for yourself? _____ Yes _____ No   a. For how long? _____ months/years

b. If yes, what type of business is it? _____

c. Business Type:   _____ Non-profit   _____ LLC   _____ INC   _____ Other _____

d. Business Location:   _____ Home based   _____ Leased Space   _____ Other _____

e. Business Address: _____

f. Are there Partners involved?   _____ Yes   _____ No   If Yes, How Many? _____

g. Company Website Address: _____

2. If no, where do you work & how long have you worked there?

_____

The Application

3. Annual Earnings/Income $_____

4. Do you have a personal checking account in good standing? ____Yes ____No

5. Name of Bank _____

6. How much money do you have in your account? $_____

    *(Would you be willing to provide proof?)_____ yes _____ no ( at a later date)*

7. Do you have a savings account in good standing? _____Yes _____No

8. How much money do you have saved? $_____

    *(Would you be willing to provide proof?) _____ yes _____ no ( at a later date)*

9. Do you have financial goals? ____Yes ____No ____Unsure

a. If yes, what are they?

_____

A Couples Guide and Workbook

b. If no, why not? _____

10. Do you have a Driver's License? _____Yes _____No

a. Is it active? (not suspended or revoked) _____Yes_____No

*(Be prepared to provide a detailed explanation)*

b. Do you have a car? _____Yes _____No

c. Make _____ Model _____ Year _____

d. Car Insurance _____ Yes _____ No

e. *If no car, how do you get around?*
_____

11. Do you own a house? _____Yes _____No

a. If yes, what is the status of the property?

_____ I live in it  ____ it is being rented  _____ unoccupied  ___don't know

The Application

12. Do you own any other real estate?  _____Yes _____No

13. Please indicate any other real estate that you own/co-own: (provide the city/state of property)

_____   _____

_____   _____

<u>14. List any/all debts:</u>

| Name of Creditor | Amount Owed | Monthly Payment Amount |
|---|---|---|
|  |  |  |
|  |  |  |
|  |  |  |
|  |  |  |
|  |  |  |
|  |  |  |

|  |  |  |
|---|---|---|
|  |  |  |
|  |  |  |
|  |  |  |

*(Use a separate sheet to continue if necessary)* Include student loans, car, credit cards, loans, furniture, etc.)

15. Do you know your credit score? _____Yes _____No

16. What is your current credit score? _____ *(Be prepared to present a copy of your credit report.)*

17. If you do not know your score, how would you describe your credit?

___excellent ___good ___fair ___poor ___I don't know

18. How often do you check your credit?

__Daily __Weekly __Monthly __Yearly ___I don't.

The Application

**ASK Your Own Question(s)**

1._____

2._____

A Couples Guide and Workbook

---------------------------------

## Education

1. High School Diploma _____Yes _____No   a. If yes, graduation date _____

2. Name of High School you attended: _____

3. College _____Yes _____No   a. If yes, did you graduate? _____

4. Name of Institution(s) you attended: _____

5. Indicate any degree(s) ___Bachelor ___Master ___PhD ___ Other _____

a. *If you do not have a degree*, are you enrolled now? _____Yes _____No

6. Do you plan to enroll? _____Yes _____No

7. Choice of Major_____

8. When do you anticipate graduating? _____ (year)

The Application

9. Do you hold any professional license or certificate? _____Yes _____No

a. In what? _____

**ASK Your Own Question(s)**

1._____

2._____

A Couples Guide and Workbook

------------------------------------------

# Family

1. Mother's Name _____

_____Biological _____Step _____ other


2. Father's Name _____

_____Biological _____Step _____ other


3. Are your parents living or deceased? _____ _____

                                      Mother                      Father

4. If deceased, how long? _____ _____

                          Mother                      Father


a. If living, what are their ages? _____ _____

                                Mother                      Father


b. Are your parents incapacitated or require assistance? _____Yes _____No

*If yes, what kind of assistance?* _____


5. Please describe your relationship with your parents:

The Application

_____

6. Any Siblings? _____Yes _____No

7. Name(s) & Age(s)

a. _____  c. _____

b. _____  d. _____

8. Please describe your relationship with your siblings:

_____

9. Were you spanked as a child? _____Yes _____No

10. Do you think it is ever okay to spank a child? _____Yes _____No

a. Why or why not?
_____

_____

11. Have you witnessed a parent or other adult being abused? ____Yes _____No

*(If yes, be prepared to discuss.)*

12. Do you have contact with extended family members? ____Yes _____No

**ASK Your Own Question(s)**

1._____

2._____

The Application

------------------------------------------------

# Marital/Child Rearing Perspectives

1. Have you ever been married? _____ Yes _____ No

2. Former/Ex-spouse Name_____

a. Reason the relationship ended: _____

*(Be prepared to discuss.)*

3. Her/His Location _____

                                  City                 State

4. If yes, how long were you married? _____ date (month/year)

5. Who filed for the divorce? _____ self _____ the other person

a. Give a brief explanation for the divorce:_____

_____

# A Couples Guide and Workbook

_____

*(Be prepared to discuss.)*

6. When was the divorced finalized? _____ (month/year)

7. Did the marriage produce any children? ____Yes ____No

a. If yes, how many? _____

b. Names/Age(s) of child(ren) _____

_____

c. Are any children deceased?  ____Yes ____No

If yes, name(s) and how long ago? _____

8. Do you have any other children? _____Yes _____No

a. If yes, how many? _____

*(Be prepared to provide details & discuss.)*

b. Age(s) of child(ren) _____

c. If no, do you want to have children? _____Yes _____No

The Application

d. If yes, how many? _____ when? _____

9. Is there a court ordered child support agreement in place? _____Yes _____No

a. OR  Do you pay child support independently? _____Yes _____No

10. How often/ how much? _____

11. Have you ever been late paying child support? _____Yes _____No

*(If yes, be prepared to discuss.)*

a. If yes, how much do you currently owe?_____

12. Would it be okay to speak with ex-spouse/other ex-partners concerning you? ___yes ___no

a. If no, why not?
_____

_____

**ASK Your Own Question(s)**

A Couples Guide and Workbook

1._____

2._____

The Application

------------------------------------

# Spirituality/Beliefs

1. When did you commit your life to righteousness or a higher being? _____ (month/year)

a. In what city? _____

b. Name of Your Place of Worship/Belief/Practice _____

2. Have you ever been excommunicated? ____Yes ____No   a. How long? _____

3. When? (month/year) _____

4. What was the reason(s)? _____

*(Be prepared to provide details.)*

5. Have you ever just stopped participating/attending service? ____Yes ____No

a. How long? ____

6. When ?(month/year) _____

7. What was the reason(s)? _____

_____

*(Be prepared to provide details.)*

8. Have you held any spiritual position(s) before? _____Yes _____No

9. Position(s) Held:

_____    _____

a. How long did you hold the position(s)? _____

10. Do you currently hold a position? _____Yes _____No

a.) Title/Role: _____

11. How often do you attend service/fellowship? _____

12. How often do you pay charity? _____ Amount $_____

The Application

13. How many relationships/courtships have you been in since joining or affiliating with this group/organization/church/mosque/belief system? _____(actual number)


14. How many did not end in marriage? _____ *(Be prepared to discuss & provide details.)*


15. Do you complete daily prayers? ___Yes ___ Sometimes ___No


16. Do you study the spiritual/ethical scripture? ____Yes ____ Sometimes ____No


17. Do you like to read? ____Yes ____ Sometimes ____No


18. Name some of your favorite reading materials:


Book/Author

_____    _____

_____    _____

_____    _____

_____          _____

24. How important is propagating your beliefs to you and why?

_____

_____

*(Be prepared to discuss.)*

**ASK Your Own Question(s)**

1._____

2._____

The Application

-------------------------------------

# Criminal Record

1. Have you ever been charged & convicted of a crime(s)? _____Yes _____No

a. If yes, what was the charge(s)?_____

*(Be prepared to provide details)*

b. In what state(s) were you convicted? _____

c. What was you age at that time? _____

2. Were incarcerated? _____Yes_____No

a. If yes, how long were you incarcerated? _____

3. When were you released? _____ (month/year)

4. How many times have you been incarcerated? _____ *(In other words, are you a repeat offender?)* _____Yes _____No

5. Have any members of your family been incarcerated? _____Yes _____No

a. If yes, when? _____ (year) b. Reason(s) for incarceration?

_____

c. How many? _____ (*if more than one family member, please be prepared for further discussion*).

d. Your relationship to the incarcerated family member(s)?

_____

7. Currently, are there any members of your family incarcerated? _____Yes _____No

a. If yes, when? _____ (year) b. Reason(s) for incarceration?

_____

c. How many? _____ (*if more than one family member, please be prepared for further discussion*)

d. Your relationship to the incarcerated family member(s)?

The Application

_____

8. Any current outstanding warrants? _____ Yes _____ No

*(If yes, please be prepared for further discussion.)*

**ASK Your Own Question(s)**

1._____

2._____

A Couples Guide and Workbook

---------------------------------

# Emotional Stability

1. How would you describe your emotional state overall?

___Very happy  ___Happy  ___Somewhat Happy  ___Unhappy  ___Very Unhappy

2. What makes you joyful, happy or feel excited and energetic?

_____   _____

_____   _____

3. What makes you feel sad, unhappy or less excited and less energetic?

_____   _____

_____   _____

4. What are some things you are passionate about?

_____   _____

The Application

_____    _____

5. What are you willing to fight for?

_____    _____

_____    _____

6. What are you willing to give your life for?

_____    _____

_____    _____

7. Have you ever been to a Counselor? ___Yes ___No ____Unsure

a. If yes, how long ago? _____

8. What was/were your reason(s) for receiving counseling?

_____    _____

_____    _____

9. Have you ever participated in any type of group counseling or therapy?

__Yes __No __Unsure   a. If yes, how long ago? _____

10. What was/were your reason(s) for participating in group counseling or therapy?

_____     _____

_____     _____

11. How did your last relationship end?

___Very happy  ___Happy  ____Somewhat Happy  ____Unhappy  ____Very Unhappy

12. Have you ever been involved in a physical altercation?

___Yes  ___No  ___Maybe

a. If yes, identify the date of your last physical altercation. _____

13. What was your relationship to the individual you had the altercation with?

_____Sibling       _____ Friend     _____ Former Spouse    _____Parent

_____Child        _____Stranger    _____Religious Official

_____ Other _____

The Application

14. What was the reason(s) for the altercation?

_____

_____

15. What was the outcome?

_____

_____

16. Do you feel that you won? ____Yes ____No ____Maybe *(Please be prepared to explain your response.)*

_____

_____

17. Have you been involved in a "heated" verbal exchange? ____ Yes ____ No

a. If yes, identify the date of your last verbal altercation._____

18. What was your relationship to the individual you had the verbal altercation with?

_____ Sibling      _____ Friend      _____ Former Spouse      _____ Parent

_____ Child        _____ Stranger    _____ Religious Official

_____ Other _____

19. What was the reason(s) for the altercation?

_____

_____

20. What was the outcome?

_____

_____

21. Do you feel that you won? ____Yes ____No ____Maybe *(Please explain your response.)*

_____

The Application

_____

22. Do you fight fair? ____Yes ____No ____Maybe

23. What do you consider evidence that you "fight" fair?

_____   _____

_____   _____

24. Identify some steps you plan to use to avoid future physical conflicts.

_____   _____

_____   _____

25. Identify some steps you plan to use to avoid future verbal conflicts.

_____   _____

_____   _____

26. Rate Your Sense of Humor:

_____ I love to Laugh           _____ I generally find Many things funny

_____ I find Some things funny   _____ I find certain things funny


27. Do you like to tell jokes? \_\_\_\_\_ Yes \_\_\_\_\_ No _____ Sometimes

a. Do you consider yourself funny? \_\_\_\_\_ Yes \_\_\_\_\_ No _____ Sometimes


**ASK Your Own Question(s)**

1._____

2._____

The Application

-------------------------------------

## Health/Sexuality

1. When was your last physical exam? _____

2. Describe your current state of health:

___excellent ___good ___fair __ poor __ I don't know

3. How often do you visit the doctor?

___monthly  ____every 3 to 6 months  ___ every 6 months to a year

____ when in serious pain   ___ I don't go to the doctor, I treat myself.

4. Do you work out? _____Yes  _____No  ____ Sometimes

How often? _____

5. What types of exercise(s)?

_____   _____

A Couples Guide and Workbook

_____          _____

_____          _____

6. How old were you when you lost your virginity? _____

7. Did you loose your virginity with a ____friend ____lover____ don't know

8. Did you loose your virginity due to an act of ____violence ___ rape ____ neither

9. Estimate how many sexual partners you have had in your life _____ (actual #)

10. Describe your sexual appetite:

____ extremely high      ____very high       ____ moderate to high

____ moderate       _____ low       _____ other _____

*(Be prepared to discuss. Other questions may be asked about sexual preferences.)*

11. Have you ever had a homosexual experience? _____Yes _____No

a. If yes, how long ago? _____ b. How long did the sexual relationship last? _____

The Application

12. Do you (or have you ever) masturbate?

___Yes ___No  a. How often? _____

b. Use sex toys? _____Yes _____No  c. Bondage sex? _____Yes _____No

d. Use pornography? _____Yes _____No  e. Kiddie porn? _____Yes _____No

f. Had a sexual relationship with underage person (under 18)? _____Yes _____No

*(If yes, be prepared to discuss.)*

13. Have you ever had any type of venereal/sexually transmitted disease? ____Yes ____No

*(If yes, be prepared to discuss.)*

*Check any and all that apply:*

____ Hep A,B or C _____Chlamdyia _____Gonorrhea _____Genital Warts

_____ Other _____ *(Be prepared to discuss details)*

14. How long ago? _____ (weeks, months, years)

a. Were you treated? ___Yes ___No

15. Have you ever had a HIV/AIDS test? _____Yes _____No

a. How long ago? _____

16. What were the results? _____

a. If positive, are you receiving treatment/counseling? _____Yes _____No

17. Have you ever been raped? _____Yes _____No

a. If yes, did you receiving counseling or attend therapy? _____Yes _____No

18. Do you or have you ever consumed alcohol? _____Yes _____No

a. If yes, what kind(s)? _____

19. Do you or have you ever used any type of illegal drugs/substances?

_____Yes _____No

# The Application

a. If yes, what kind(s)?
_____


20. Have you ever experienced depression? _____Yes _____No


a. If yes, did you seek help (counseling)? _____Yes _____No


21. Do you have any friends? _____Yes _____No


a. If no, why not?
_____

_____


b. If yes, please list their contact information here:

(They will not be contacted without your permission)


Name                           Phone #


1. _____     _____


2. _____     _____

3. _____    _____

22. Do you sleep with any of the following?

___ a night light    ___ a stuffed animal    ___ television on    ___ radio on

_____ other _____

23. Do you suffer from insomnia? _____Yes    _____No

a. If yes, have you sought treatment? _____Yes    _____No

24. When was the last time you visited a dentist? _____
                                                                    (month/year)

25. How often do you brush your teeth?_____

26. How often do you bathe? _____

27. History of known Family illnesses:

## The Application

| |
|---|
| Animal-Related Diseases |
| _____ Yes _____ No   How related? _____ |
| Bioterrorism Agents/Diseases |
| _____ Yes _____ No   How related? _____ |
| Childhood Diseases |
| _____ Yes _____ No   How related? _____ |
| Drug Resistant Infections |
| _____ Yes _____ No   How related? _____ |
| Emerging Infectious Diseases |
| _____ Yes _____ No   How related? _____ |
| Food-Related Diseases |
| _____ Yes _____ No   How related? _____ |
| Healthcare-Related Infections and Issues |
| _____ Yes _____ No   How related? _____ |
| HIV/AIDS |
| _____ Yes _____ No   How related? _____ |
| Insects and Arthropod-Related Diseases |
| _____ Yes _____ No   How related? _____ |
| Sexually Transmitted Diseases |
| _____ Yes _____ No   How related? _____ |

| |
|---|
| Tuberculosis (TB) |
| _____ Yes _____ No  How related? _____ |
| Water-Related Diseases |
| _____ Yes _____ No  How related? _____ |
| Bleeding Disorders |
| _____ Yes _____ No  How related? _____ |
| Arthritis |
| _____ Yes _____ No  How related? _____ |
| Asthma & Allergies |
| _____ Yes _____ No  How related? _____ |
| Cancer |
| _____ Yes _____ No  How related? _____ |
| Chronic Fatigue Syndrome |
| _____ Yes _____ No  How related? _____ |
| Diabetes |
| _____ Yes _____ No  How related? _____ |
| Epilepsy |
| _____ Yes _____ No  How related? _____ |
| Heart Disease |
| _____ Yes _____ No  How related? _____ |

## The Application

| |
|---|
| Hepatitis B |
| _____ Yes  _____ No  How related? _____ |
| Hepatitis C |
| _____ Yes  _____ No  How related? _____ |
| Iron Overload |
| _____ Yes  _____ No  How related? _____ |
| Osteoporosis |
| _____ Yes  _____ No  How related? _____ |
| Overweight and Obesity |
| _____ Yes  _____ No  How related? _____ |
| Stroke |
| _____ Yes  _____ No  How related? _____ |
| *[Categories retrieved December 21, 2011 from http://www.cdc.gov/]* |

**ASK Your Own Question(s)**

1. _____

2. _____

3. _____

A Couples Guide and Workbook

The Application

# Writing Activity

The purpose of this section is to provide insight regarding the sometimes intangible and illusive dynamics that reflect your ability to be introspective about your ideas, intents and purpose.

*Utilizing a separate sheet of paper complete the following:*

- 5 life goals/plans/5 spiritual goals/5 economic goals that you want to achieve in the next couple of years
- Any Positive personality traits about yourself
- Any Negative personality traits about yourself
- Major things you are <u>looking for</u> in a spouse
    - spiritually
    - financially
    - emotionally
    - intellectually
    - sexually
    - physically (appearance)
    - any other things
- Major things you can <u>offer</u> to a spouse
    - spiritually
    - financially
    - emotionally
    - intellectually
    - sexually
    - physically (appearance)
    - any other things

**STOP**

RETURN to Application Instructions.
FOLLOW 2nd, 3rd, and 4th Steps in the Instruction pages 40 - 44.

## *Epilogue*

When I begin writing *The Application*, little did I know, it would take on a life of its own. About five years ago, I was approached to be in a courtship.

Standing before me was an opportunity to use what I had taught about in class and professional presentations for over 15 years.

I knew that this time, I was going to do things differently.

I knew that this time, I had to consider three additional important dynamics: my children.

I said to myself, right then and there, that if this person was serious about a long-term commitment, than they would have to not only commit to me but to my children.

The person I would marry must also love my children; in fact, he must love them more than he loves me. After all, we have no control over when we come to this life nor when we leave and I had to be sure that, the individual was capable of caring for and securing my children.

For me, *The Application* is personal. It is not a game or joke and I do not take the process of commitment lightly. Neither should you.

## *Definition of Terms*

**Application**: a form completed as part of a process to determine the value, status, and possible acceptance of a person for a particular role, function, and/or purpose.

**Character**: the actions and behavior that give meaning to a persons desire, intention and will.

**Characteristics**: the traits determined to be reflective of character.

**Courtship**: the practice of critical assessment for a long term committed relationship, i.e., marriage. Typically involves structured meeting and get-togethers.

**Dating**: the practice of going on a date. To associate with someone with no established intention of a long-term commitment, i.e. marriage.

**Engagement**: an agreement to marry. Typified when persons determine that they are ready to proceed toward marriage.

**Independent**: to exist without the need or requirement of another person or entity. Typified in a relationship as someone who is able to support and sustain his or herself socially, emotionally, spiritually, intellectually, sexually and financially.

**Intention**: purpose and motive for actions and behaviors. Also the reason related to and associated with outcome and results.

## The Application

**Interview**: a process by which individuals engage one another to determine mutual interest, ideas, roles and status. Usually involves specific and detailed open-ended questions.

**Introspective**: a process by which one reflects upon one's own self to ascertain self-identity, self-values, self-conception and self-motivation.

**Interrogation**: an aggressive and forceful manner used to obtain information from a person. Involves harsh, threatening techniques and manipulative tactics to force and obtain responses from an individual during questioning.

**Mate**: a status that describes an individual who has accepted a supportive role in a relationship to another. Typified by emotional, spiritual, intellectual, social, sexual and financial commitments.

**Marriage**: a legal binding contract of commitment. A process of reaching total fulfillment and duty toward another person. To bind one's interest to another. An agreement to support a person socially, emotionally, intellectually, sexually and financially.

**Reconcile**: to bring into agreement, in line with a particular idea, value, and or perspectives. To settle differences and/or disagreements.

**Relationship**: describes the way and manner that people associate and form partnerships based on perceived benefits and idealized agreements.

## *Suggested Book Readings*

Ali, Betty (2011) Nursing Your Marriage

Chapman, Gary D. (2010) The 5 Love Languages: The Secret to Love That Lasts

Fisher, Helen (2009) Why Him? Why Her

Gray, John (2007) Men Are from Mars, Women Are from Venus: The Classic Guide to Understanding the Opposite Sex

Hafeezah, General (2010) Before You Say "I Do" His/Hers

Harris, Joshua (2000, 2005) Boy Meets Girl

Hendrix, Harville (2007) Getting the Love You Want

Muhammad, Ava (1997) Real Love

Real, Terrence (2007) The New Rules of Marriage

## Notes

## ABOUT THE AUTHOR

Dr. Toni Sims-Muhammad began her teaching career over 20 years ago and has taught at several institutions in the United States including Grambling State University, Georgia Perimeter College, Western Illinois University, University of Phoenix, the University of Louisiana at Lafayette and Livingstone College. Some of her teaching, research interest and expertise are in marriage and the family, social class and social stratification, race and ethnicity, black studies, black women in American society, and multiculturalism.

http://www.tonisimsmuhammad.com

www.ingramcontent.com/pod-product-compliance
Lightning Source LLC
LaVergne TN
LVHW061345060426
835512LV00012B/2576